The Big Little Golden Book of
FUNNY POEMS

Selected by Thea Feldman
Illustrated by Bruce Lemerise

A Golden Book • New York
Western Publishing Company, Inc., Racine, Wisconsin 53404

Laughing Time

It was laughing time, and the tall Giraffe
Lifted his head, and began to laugh:

Ha! Ha!   Ha! Ha!

And the Chimpanzee on the ginkgo tree
Swung merrily down with a *Tee Hee Hee*:

Hee! Hee!   Hee! Hee!

"It's certainly not against the law!"
Croaked Justice Crow with a loud guffaw:

Haw! Haw!   Haw! Haw!

The dancing Bear who could never say "No"
Waltzed up and down on the tip of his toe:

Ho! Ho!   Ho! Ho!

The Donkey daintily took his paw,
And around they went: Hee-Haw! Hee-Haw!

Hee-Haw!   Hee-Haw!

The Moon had to smile as it started to climb;
All over the world it was laughing time!

Ho! Ho!   Ho! Ho!   Hee-Haw!   Hee-Haw!
Hee! Hee!   Hee! Hee!   Ha! Ha!   Ha! Ha!

William Jay Smith

The Time Has Come

"The time has come," the Walrus said,
  "To talk of many things:
Of shoes—and ships—and sealing-wax—
  Of cabbages—and kings—
And why the sea is boiling hot—
  And whether pigs have wings."

Lewis Carroll

Timothy

Timothy likes
To stand on his head
And think of the wonderful
Books he has read
He can juggle five books
On the tips of his toes
While he brushes his teeth
And scratches his nose.

Arnold Spilka

I Asked My Mother

I asked my mother for fifty cents
To see the elephant jump the fence.
He jumped so high that he touched the sky
And never came back till the Fourth of July.

Friendly Fredrick Fuddlestone

Friendly Fredrick Fuddlestone
Could fiddle on his funny bone.
When Freddy fiddled
    foolishly fast,
He found his father
    frankly aghast.
Friendly Fredrick Fuddlestone
Kept fiddling on his funny bone.
His furious father
    would flatly forbid it,
Which, of course,
    is why young Freddy did it.

Arnold Lobel

Daddy Fell into the Pond

Everyone grumbled. The sky was grey.
We had nothing to do and nothing to say.
We were nearing the end of a dismal day,
And there seemed to be nothing beyond,
                    THEN
   Daddy fell into the pond!

And everyone's face grew merry and bright,
And Timothy danced for sheer delight.
"Give me the camera, quicky, oh quick!
He's crawling out of the duckweed."
   Click!

Then the gardener suddenly slapped his knee,
And doubled up, shaking silently,
And the ducks all quacked as if they were daft,
And it sounded as if the old drake laughed.

O, there wasn't a thing that didn't respond
                    WHEN
   Daddy fell into the pond!

Alfred Noyes

She Sells Seashells

She sells seashells on the seashore.
The shells she sells are seashells, I'm sure.
So if she sells seashells on the seashore,
I'm sure she sells seashore shells.

A Skunk Sat on a Stump

A skunk sat on a stump.
The skunk thinked
the stump stunk,
but the stump thunk
the skunk stunk.

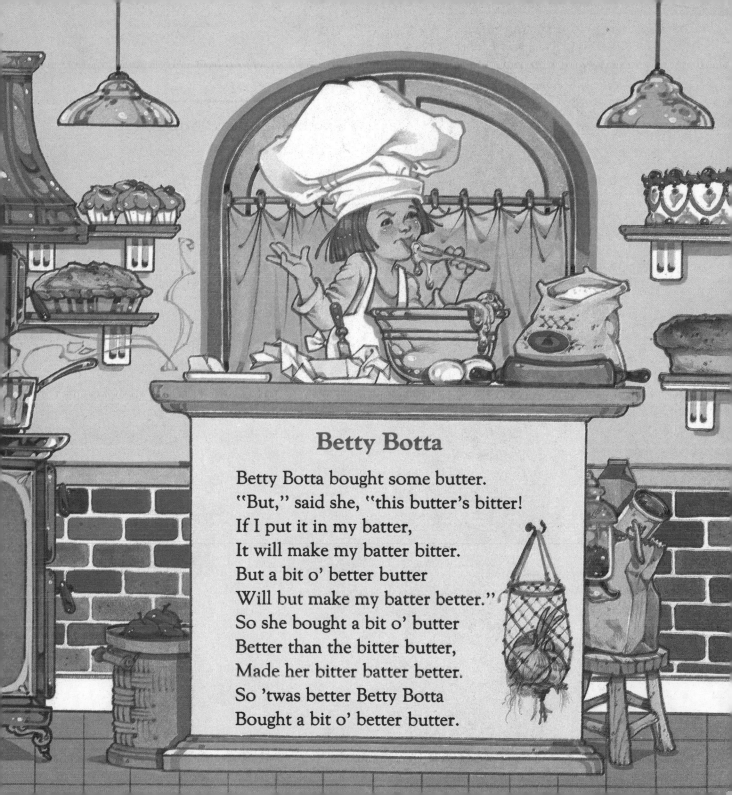

Betty Botta

Betty Botta bought some butter.
"But," said she, "this butter's bitter!
If I put it in my batter,
It will make my batter bitter.
But a bit o' better butter
Will but make my batter better."
So she bought a bit o' butter
Better than the bitter butter,
Made her bitter batter better.
So 'twas better Betty Botta
Bought a bit o' better butter.

Song of the Pop-Bottlers

Pop bottles pop-bottles
  In pop shops;
The pop-bottles Pop bottles
  Poor Pop drops.

When Pop drops pop-bottles,
  Pop-bottles plop!
Pop-bottle-tops topple!
  Pop mops slop!

Stop! Pop'll drop bottle!
  Stop, Pop, stop!
When Pop bottles pop-bottles,
  Pop-bottles pop!

Morris Bishop

So Many Monkeys

Monkey Monkey Moo!
Shall we buy a few?
Yellow monkeys,
Purple monkeys,
Monkeys red and blue.

Be a monkey, do!
Who's a monkey, *who*?
He's a monkey,
She's a monkey,
You're a monkey, too!

Marion Edey and Dorothy Grider

Boing! Boing! Squeak!

Boing! Boing! squeak!
Boing! Boing! squeak!
A bouncing mouse is in my house,
it's been here for a week.

It bounced from out of nowhere,
then quickly settled in,
I'm grateful that it came alone
(I've heard it has a twin),
it bounces in the kitchen,
it bounces in the den,
it bounces through the living room—
look! There it goes again.

Boing! Boing! squeak!
Boing! Boing! squeak!
A bouncing mouse is in my house,
it's been here for a week.

It bounces on the sofa,
on the table and the bed,
up the stairs and on the chairs
and even on my head,
that mouse continues bouncing
every minute of the day,
it bounces, bounces, bounces,
but it doesn't bounce away.

Boing! Boing! squeak!
Boing! Boing! squeak!
A bouncing mouse is in my house,
it's been here for a week.

Jack Prelutsky

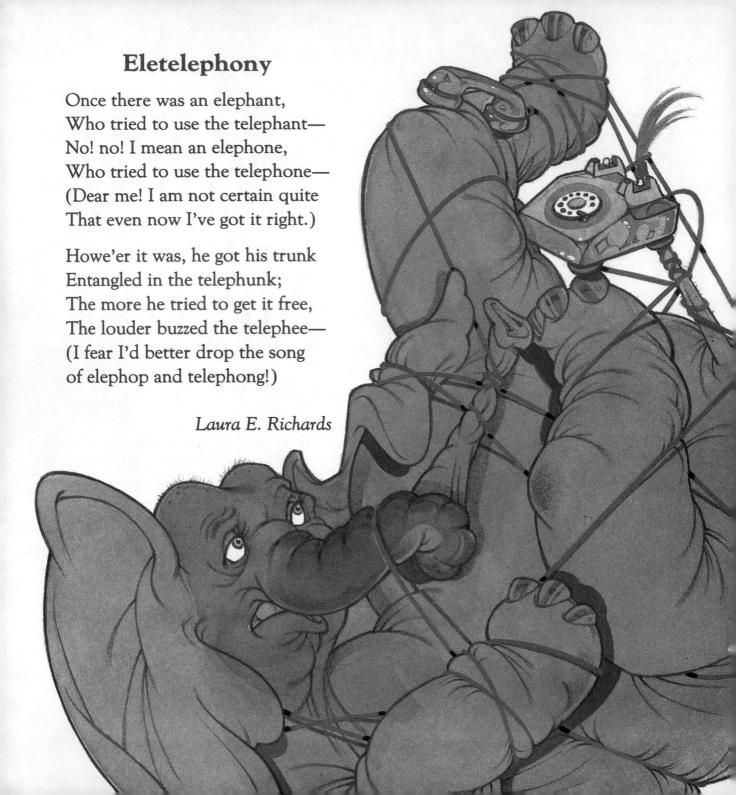

Eletelephony

Once there was an elephant,
Who tried to use the telephant—
No! no! I mean an elephone,
Who tried to use the telephone—
(Dear me! I am not certain quite
That even now I've got it right.)

Howe'er it was, he got his trunk
Entangled in the telephunk;
The more he tried to get it free,
The louder buzzed the telephee—
(I fear I'd better drop the song
of elephop and telephong!)

Laura E. Richards

Toot! Toot!

A peanut sat on a railroad track,
His heart was all a-flutter;
The five-fifteen came rushing by—
Toot! toot! peanut butter!

Lost and Found

LOST:
A Wizard's loving pet.
Rather longish.
Somewhat scaly.
May be hungry or
upset.
Please feed daily.

P.S. Reward

FOUND:
A dragon
breathing fire.
Flails his scaly
tail
in ire.
Would eat twenty LARGE meals
daily
if we let him.
PLEASE
come and get him.

P.S. No reward necessary

Lilian Moore

While Dining at Crewe

A diner while dining at Crewe
Found a rather large mouse in his stew.
  Said the waiter, "Don't shout
  And wave it about,
Or the rest will be wanting one, too."

There Was an Old Man

There was an Old Man with a beard,
Who said, "It is just as I feared!—
  Two Owls and a Hen,
  Four Larks and a Wren,
Have all built their nests in my beard!"

Edward Lear

There Was a Young Man

There was a young man from the city,
Who met what he thought was a kitty.
   He gave it a pat,
    And said, "Nice little cat!"
And they buried his clothes out of pity.

In the Motel

Bouncing! bouncing! on the beds
My brother Bob and I cracked heads—

People next door heard the crack,
Whammed on the wall, so we whammed right back.

Dad's razor caused an overload
And wow! did the TV set explode!

Someone's car backed fast and—tinkle!
In our windshield was a wrinkle.

Eight more days on the road? Hooray!
What a bang-up holiday!

X. J. Kennedy

Don't Worry

Don't worry if your job is small
And your rewards are few.
Remember that the mighty oak
Was once a nut like you.

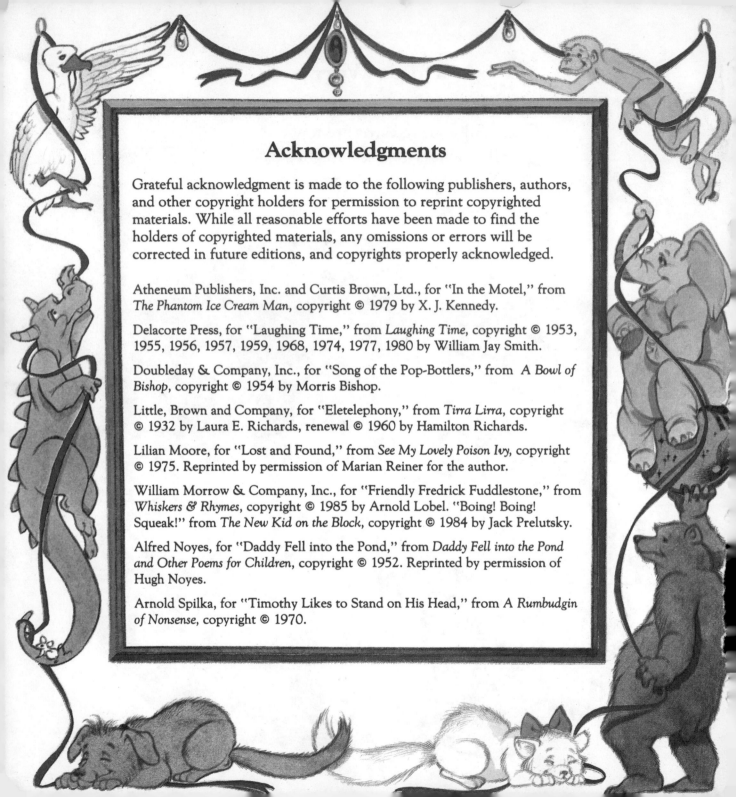

Acknowledgments

Grateful acknowledgment is made to the following publishers, authors, and other copyright holders for permission to reprint copyrighted materials. While all reasonable efforts have been made to find the holders of copyrighted materials, any omissions or errors will be corrected in future editions, and copyrights properly acknowledged.

Atheneum Publishers, Inc. and Curtis Brown, Ltd., for "In the Motel," from *The Phantom Ice Cream Man*, copyright © 1979 by X. J. Kennedy.

Delacorte Press, for "Laughing Time," from *Laughing Time*, copyright © 1953, 1955, 1956, 1957, 1959, 1968, 1974, 1977, 1980 by William Jay Smith.

Doubleday & Company, Inc., for "Song of the Pop-Bottlers," from *A Bowl of Bishop*, copyright © 1954 by Morris Bishop.

Little, Brown and Company, for "Eletelephony," from *Tirra Lirra*, copyright © 1932 by Laura E. Richards, renewal © 1960 by Hamilton Richards.

Lilian Moore, for "Lost and Found," from *See My Lovely Poison Ivy*, copyright © 1975. Reprinted by permission of Marian Reiner for the author.

William Morrow & Company, Inc., for "Friendly Fredrick Fuddlestone," from *Whiskers & Rhymes*, copyright © 1985 by Arnold Lobel. "Boing! Boing! Squeak!" from *The New Kid on the Block*, copyright © 1984 by Jack Prelutsky.

Alfred Noyes, for "Daddy Fell into the Pond," from *Daddy Fell into the Pond and Other Poems for Children*, copyright © 1952. Reprinted by permission of Hugh Noyes.

Arnold Spilka, for "Timothy Likes to Stand on His Head," from *A Rumbudgin of Nonsense*, copyright © 1970.